MORE

Old Jokes

for Old Folks

....

Giggles for Geezers

Publications International, Ltd.

Holli Fort, having shared her adult life with four grandparents and one great-grandmother, can appreciate the wisdom and humor that comes with age. And as the mother of three young sons, she definitely needs it!

Angela Hampt-Sanchez is a mother of seven and the delighted grandmother of seven with two more grandchildren on the way. An extensive traveler, she makes sure that her sense of humor is always right at hand (keeping it in the car itself, not packed away in the trunk).

Finding themselves jobless in their early 60s, **Frank and Carolyn Kaiser** of Clearwater, Florida, began writing their international column, *Suddenly Senior*—the daily e-zine for everyone over 50 who feels way too young to be old. Eleven years later, it's read by 3.1 million in 83 newspapers and magazines around the world (www.suddenlysenior.com).

Comedy writer **Paul Seaburn** believes that laughter keeps him young, no matter what his driver's license photo implies. Paul writes comedy for television, radio, the Internet, humor books, magazines, and comedians. He's the head writer for a jazz-blues-and-comedy show on public radio and has more info and laughs at www.humorhandyman.com.

Illustrations: Shutterstock.com/Dennis Cox

Louis Weber, CEO
Publications International, Ltd.
8140 Lehigh Avenue
Morton Grove, Illinois 60053

ISBN-13: 978-1-4508-1717-2
ISBN-10: 1-4508-1717-3

Manufactured in U.S.A.

8 7 6 5 4 3 2 1

Contents

. . . .

Growing Old Might Not Be Fun, but It Sure Can Be Funny!

• • • • • • • • • • • • • • • •

"Mature" is great for cheeses and wines, but sometimes it's good to let the kid inside us have some fun. Since we're not getting any younger, why not look for the comedy gold in the golden years? *More Old Jokes for Old Folks: Giggles for Geezers* is designed to help us all remember that we may lose our teeth, but good humor still has a sharp bite. With humor taken from everyday situations and unique experiences alike, these jokes will remind you that you may be retired, but getting old is still funny business.

When I Had Snapper in My Whipper

. . . .

Debbie and Phil were sitting in the living room watching the tube when he said to her, "Just so you know, I never want to live in a vegetative state, dependent on some machine and fluids from a bottle. If that ever happens, just pull the plug."

She got up, unplugged the TV, and threw his beer out the window!

*   *   *

The Post Office finally had to retire my grandpa; he had really lost his zip.

*   *   *

It hurt when you first noticed that it had been a while since you were asked for I.D. to purchase alcohol.

Now it hurts because you realize it has been a while since anyone has asked you to show your I.D. to receive the Senior Special Discount.

*   *   *

Denture Venture

A boy goes to spend the night with his grandparents. His grandfather goes to bed early, but his grandmother wants to stay up and watch a movie with him.

She sends the boy upstairs to put on his pajamas. When the boy comes down, his eyes are as big as saucers.

"I looked in your bedroom on the way down, and now I know why Grandpa was so happy to go to sleep early. Boy, the Tooth Fairy is going to be surprised tonight when she sees what he left on his nightstand!"

* * *

"Why didn't someone tell me that when you get older, you go through the terrible twos again? Now I've got two chins, two spare tires, and two really big ears."

* * *

Four retired guys are walking down a street in Chicago when they turn a corner and a see a sign that says, "Old Timers' Bar. ALL DRINKS: Ten Cents!"

They look at each other, and then go in. The old bartender says, "What'll it be, gentlemen?"

It seems to be a fully stocked bar, so the four men each ask for a martini. In short order, the bartender serves up four iced martinis and says, "That'll be ten cents each, please."

They can't believe their good luck, plunking down four dimes.

Finally, one of the men can't stand it any longer and asks the bartender, "How can you afford to serve martinis as good as these for a dime each?"

"Well, I always wanted to own a bar. Last year, I hit the lottery for $25 million and opened this place. Every drink costs a dime—wine, liquor, beer, all the same."

"WOW!! That's something," says one of the men. The four of them can't help but notice three old guys at the end of the bar who don't have drinks and aren't ordering anything.

"What's with them?"

The bartender says, "Oh, they're seniors up from Florida. They are *still* waiting for half-off happy hour."

*   *   *

An elderly gentleman is attending a singles mixer at a senior center, and he approaches a woman to speak to her.

At a loss for words, he falls back on what seems to be one of his old standbys: "So tell me, do I come here often?"

*   *   *

What Was That Question Again?

An extremely elderly couple had been dating for over six years. The gentleman finally decided to ask his girlfriend to marry him.

She immediately accepted his proposal.

He went home happy. The next morning, however, he couldn't remember not only her answer, but also whether or not he had actually asked her. Very awkward indeed!

He drank almost an entire pot of coffee trying to remember, but it was no use, he would have to call her and ask her outright, as embarrassing as it would be.

"Oh, I am so glad you called," she exclaimed. "I remembered saying 'yes' to someone about something, but I couldn't remember to whom or about what!"

* * *

They gave me a watch when I retired, which was useless since it was the first time I didn't need to follow a schedule in my life. Since I go to Starbucks in the morning now, what I *really* could have used was an English-to-*coffeehouse* dictionary!

Now I may never know what a *skinny frappa-latta-chino* is.

* * *

Forget those big-and-tall stores for men and mature-figure shops for women.

At my age, I need a short-and-stooped shop: someplace where I can get a shirt that's long in the back, short in the sleeves, and has one big button in the front that I can see without my glasses.

* * *

It's obvious that the people who make those little bottles of that stuff you add to beans to cut flatulence aren't senior citizens.

If they were, that stuff would come in a keg with a spigot!

* * *

Senior citizen cruises are not for me. If I want to see a bunch of old people hanging over the rail and tossing their lunches, I'll go to all-you-can-eat day at the racetrack.

* * *

The Sum of Her Parts

Helen went in for a doctor's appointment, and was told she should probably have her knee replaced. The news sent her into a tizzy.

"What do you mean, have my knee replaced? I've already had both hips replaced, one knee replaced, and a heart valve replaced. Even my teeth have been replaced. Pretty soon, there will be nothing left of me!

"Anything else you want to replace, *doctor,* or will this do it?"

As she got upset, Helen's face got more and more red, and she began to sweat.

"Well, while we're on the subject, we might think about replacing some of those hormones...."

* * *

Doctor's Orders!

A woman accompanied her elderly husband to his doctor's appointment. After a thorough examination, the doctor took the wife to his office to speak privately with her.

"If you don't follow my instructions carefully, your husband may not have long to live. Every morning, wake him gently with a nice back rub, make him fresh squeezed orange juice, and only prepare his favorite foods at all meals, in the healthiest ways possible. Read the newspaper to him, and allow him to play golf as much as he likes. Never bother him with problems or ask him to help around the house. Draw him a warm bath every night, and as you tuck him into bed, give him a foot rub to end the day."

On the car ride home, the husband asked his wife what the doctor had said.

She replied, "We need to make sure your will is in order."

* * *

My old pal Gus is always trying to outdo me. Yesterday, I showed him the little plastic pill case with compartments I use for all of my medications.

Today, he showed me the *tackle box* he uses for his.

*   *   *

In church one day, the sermon was about Moses wandering through the desert for 40 years.

Charlene leaned over and whispered loudly to the woman next to her:

"Moses has something in common with my husband; I've seen him wandering for 40 years, and he never stops to ask for directions either!"

You know you're old when your résumé goes back to your days as an abacus repair technician.

"Yoga" must have been named by an old monk, because that's the same sound I make when trying to get up off the floor after doing yoga.

One great thing about getting old is that you can get out of all sorts of social obligations just by saying you're too tired.

—GEORGE CARLIN

*　　*　　*

Over a number of months, a wife noticed her husband was suddenly obsessed with the daily paper's obituary section. One morning, she asked, "Dear, are you getting afraid that you're going to die?"

The indignant reply came: "No way! I'm just trying to get a good idea of who will and won't be at the class reunion!"

*　　*　　*

Well, now that I am old enough to watch my step, I don't go anywhere that I need to.

*　　*　　*

An older gentleman was on the operating table awaiting surgery, and he insisted that his son, a renowned surgeon, perform the operation. As he was about to get the anesthesia, he asked to speak to his son.

"Yes, Dad, what is it?"

"Don't be nervous, son; do your best. Just remember, if it doesn't go well, if something happens to me, your mother is going to come and live with you and your wife...."

* * *

Like a lot of fellows around here, I have a furniture problem. My chest has fallen into my drawers.

—BILLY CASPER

* * *

On a cross-country flight, an older woman started to panic. Having located a doctor to help her, the flight attendant warned the doctor that the woman was a little hard of hearing. The doctor approached the woman.

"Ma'am, I'm a doctor, and I'm going to help you get through this."

"What's that?"

"I SAID I'M GOING TO HELP YOU THROUGH THIS. NOW, BIG BREATHS."

"Well, they used to be, anyway," the woman replied sadly.

* * *

The View Is a Little Different from Here

A very short, very elderly woman calls 911, hysterically reporting that her old Oldsmobile has been broken into, and it has been ransacked.

"It's terrible, everything has been dismantled and stolen. The stereo, the steering wheel, the brake pedal, why even the gas pedal is missing," she cried.

"Okay, try to calm down, an officer will be there any moment, and I will stay on the phone with you until he arrives."

Just moments later the officer gets on the phone and tells the dispatcher, "Yeah, go ahead and cancel this call. She got in the back door by mistake is all, and couldn't see over the seat."

* * *

On the occasion of her late-in-life third wedding, Betty was given a party by her closest friends. When it came time for the toast, her best friend stood up to speak.

"We all know how happy Betty is going to be this time around. She's finally found the love of her life. Not to mention that she's finally taken to heart the best advice I ever gave her: 'You must always marry for the money, honey—a rich man's joke is always funny!'"

* * *

Enjoying a post-workout smoothie, four friends sat around comparing their various aches and pains.

"My knees are killing me!" said the first.

"I can barely bend over, my back aches so badly," lamented the second.

"I think every one of my joints is swollen," the third chimed in.

The fourth friend just grinned and said:

"Let's face it: The only thing that doesn't hurt about getting old is getting gray hair!"

*   *   *

You know you're getting old when you can pinch an inch on your forehead.

—JOHN MENDOZA

*   *   *

TEAM NAMES IF THE NFL ESTABLISHED A "SENIOR LEAGUE"

. . . .

- San Francisco 79ers
- Cleveland Brown Spots
- Carolina Panters
- Tampa Bay Miracle Ears
- Cincinnati Ben Gays
- Washington Dryskins
- Green Bay Backaches
- Oakland X-Rayders

They had a new game over at the retirement center, "Musical Wheelchairs."

It was great fun until folks started using those electric ones, and when they got up out of their chairs, the chairs still kept going!

✳   ✳   ✳

You know you're old when the cops stop asking if you know how fast you were going and start asking if you know *where* you were going.

* * *

At my age, I don't mind having to brush dandruff off of my shoulders.

It helps me remember to put my shirt on.

* * *

It's true, some wines improve with age, but only if the grapes were good in the first place.

—ABIGAIL VAN BUREN

* * *

Old limbo dancers never die, they just go under for the last time.

* * *

Once her husband had nagged her into getting an annual checkup, Sara reluctantly decides to open up to the doctor about her worst fear.

"Doctor, I'm really worried that I might be losing my memory."

"All right, we'll check it out. Anything else?"

"Yes. I'm really worried that I might be losing my memory."

* * *

Shop Till Ya Drop

Simon and Martha, both residents of the retirement community, are strolling around downtown, planning their wedding. As they pass a drugstore, Simon decides they should speak with the owner.

"Excuse me, are you the owner?"

The pharmacist answers, "Yes, how may I help you?"

"Do you sell heart medication?" asks Simon. "Yes, certainly," was the reply.

"What about medicine for poor circulation?" The pharmacist answers in the affirmative.

On and on Simon and Martha ask the owner of the drugstore about all the many types of medications they require, and Simon even asks if the store sells Viagra, which causes Martha to blush. In every instance, the pharmacy owner answers that he can supply all their pharmaceutical needs.

Finally, Simon seems satisfied, and turns
to Martha with this comment, "My dear,
I believe we have *finally* found the perfect
place to register for our wedding gifts."

✳   ✳   ✳

A fine old fellow fell in love with a lovely lady at his retirement center. He managed to get down on his knees in front of her, looked up, and said there were two very important things he needed to ask her.

She smiled, sure she knew the first question, but wondering what the second question was. "Okay, dear," she replied.

He asked her the hoped for question, "Shirley, will you marry me?"

"Yes, Harvey, I will! Now what is the second question?" she asked.

He replied, "Will you go get someone to help me up?"

*　　*　　*

You know you're getting old when the only rocking out you do is on a chair on your front porch.

*　　*　　*

I found a great new store for senior women called "Grandma Vickie's Secret."

It has the same stuff as the other lingerie places except the elastic has been replaced with steel cables.

* * *

Surprise!

A woman went to the doctor's office where she was seen by one of the younger doctors. After about four minutes in the examination room, she burst out, screaming as she ran down the hall.

An older doctor stopped her and asked what the problem was, and she told him her story.

After listening, he had her sit down and relax in another room. The older doctor marched down the hallway to the back where the young doctor was writing on his clipboard.

"What's the matter with you?" the older doctor demanded. "Mrs. Reid is 62 years old, has four grown children and seven grandchildren, and you told her she was pregnant?"

The younger doctor continued writing and without looking up said, "Does she still have the hiccups?"

* * *

TOP ROCK ALBUMS
MADE BY SENIORS

. . . .

- Sgt. Pepper's Lonely Hearts Club Dating Service
- Pet Sounds Other Than Farts
- Revolve Around My Grandkids
- Highway 61 is Too Dangerous
- Rubber Soles for Slippery Floors
- I Don't Care What's Going On
- Nobody Gets Exiled on Main Street Anymore
- Bottle Blonde on Bottle Blonde
- Flabby Road
- Are You Experienced and Do You Give Senior Discounts?

You don't see many senior citizens at those two-hour comedy club shows.

We don't mind laughing until we wet our pants, but what are we going to do for the other hour and 59 minutes?

* * *

I want my children to have all the things I couldn't afford. Then I want to move in with them.

—PHYLLIS DILLER

*   *   *

When I'm at the grocery store, I can always spot the seniors who just came back from the doctor.

They're the ones looking at the expiration dates on packages and yelling, "Go ahead! Rub it in!"

*   *   *

Growing old is like being increasingly penalized for a crime you haven't committed.

—ANTHONY POWELL

*   *   *

Oldies but Goodies

Three elderly men meet up for their daily walk around the neighborhood. As is their custom, they take turns airing the day's grievances.

"This morning," begins the first man, "I was so stiff and sore that it took me 15 minutes to get out of bed and hobble into the bathroom."

"That's nothing!" scoffs the second man. "I was so stiff and sore that I couldn't hobble to the bathroom for a full hour!"

"I've got you both beat," says the third man sadly. "This morning, I got up and was listening to the radio, and then I realized it was the oldies station."

"What's so bad about that?" asks the first two.

"They were playing music my grandchildren used to listen to!"

＊　　＊　　＊

Never attempt to teach your grandchildren any of the games you played when you were a kid.

I tried to teach mine how to play "Run Sheep Run," and they called PETA on me.

* * *

In an effort to preserve her stories for the next generations of her family, Dottie decided to start her own blog.

She called it "The Memory Project: Tales of . . . Where Was I Again?"

* * *

Middle age is when you have a choice of two temptations and choose the one that will get you home earlier.

—DAN BENNETT

* * *

If I Was Interested In What You're Saying, I'd Turn On My Hearing Aid

• • • • • • • • • • • • • • • •

As Margaret comes down the stairs, her daughter looks up in surprise. "Mom, you look great! Where are you headed?"

"I'm going clubbing," Margaret serenely replies.

"Really?"

"Yes. Now if I could just remember whether I'm supposed to be at book club or quilting club, I'd be all set."

✳   ✳   ✳

You know you're having a senior moment when it takes three tries to remember you're in the flower shop for forget-me-nots.

✳   ✳   ✳

There's one more terrifying fact about old people: I'm going to be one soon.

—P. J. O'ROURKE

✳   ✳   ✳

My granddaughter was bugging her parents to let her get a tattoo, so I told her I'd help if she showed me the design.

As she described the flower, I drew it on a ball of clay. Then I stretched the clay and showed her what the tattoo would look like when she reached my age.

Now she's getting her ears pierced instead.

* * *

Age is an issue of mind over matter. If you don't mind, it doesn't matter.

—MARK TWAIN

* * *

I feel sorry for my old pal Gus. He's a retired fisherman, and now he has nothing to do.

* * *

Old age is like a plane flying through a storm. Once you're abroad, there's nothing you can do.

—GOLDA MEIR

*　　*　　*

Old WWF wrestlers never die; they just really lose their grip.

*　　*　　*

Grandma In Court

Lawyers should never ask a Mississippi grandma a question if they aren't prepared for the answer. In a trial, a small-town prosecuting attorney calls his first witness, a grandmotherly woman, to the stand.

He approaches her and asks, "Mrs. Jones, do you know me?"

She responds, "Why, I do know you, Mr. Williams. I've known you since you were a boy, and frankly, you've been a big disappointment. You lie, you cheat on your wife, and you talk about folks behind their backs. You think you're a big shot, but you never amounted to anything more than a two-bit paper pusher. Yes, I know you."

Stunned, the prosecutor points across the room and asks, "Mrs. Jones, do you know the defense attorney?"

She replies, "Why, yes. I've known Mr. Bradley since he was a youngster, too. He's lazy, bigoted, and he has a drinking problem. His law practice is one of the worst in the state. Not to mention he also cheats on his wife. Yes, I know him."

The judge quickly calls both counselors to approach the bench. In a very quiet voice, the judge says:

"If either of you idiots asks her if she knows me, I'll send you to the electric chair."

＊　　＊　　＊

A senior citizen is someone who can tell you where to buy cheap jogging suits but can't tell you what jogging is.

＊　　＊　　＊

SENIOR DEFINITION
. . . .
Tablet computer: A pad of paper and a pencil

I feel as if body has gotten totally out of shape, so I got my doctor's permission to join a fitness club and start exercising. I decided to take an aerobics class for seniors.

I bent, twisted, gyrated, jumped up and down, and perspired for an hour.

But, by the time I got my leotard on, the class was over.

When I was young, "long distance" was a phone call.

Now it's the path between my chair and the bathroom.

*　*　*

I'm always relieved when someone is delivering a eulogy and I realize I'm listening to it.

—GEORGE CARLIN

*　*　*

Being retired is great! This morning, when my wife asked me what I was going to do today, I replied, "Nothing."

She said, "But honey, you did that yesterday."

"I know," I said. "But I haven't finished yet."

*　*　*

An elderly patient has been in the hospital for quite some time. He is really becoming frustrated with the care he is receiving, and he lets his doctor know it the very next time he comes by to check on him.

"Look here, Doc! You've already removed my spleen, gall bladder, tonsils, adenoids, an ingrown toenail, and one of my kidneys.

"I insist you get me out of this place!"

To which the doctor replies,

"Well, I am, bit by bit."

*　　*　　*

What do you get when Grandpa drinks his favorite soda for breakfast as a treat even though his doctor told him not to?

An early burp special.

*　　*　　*

A pair of old friends met up at the senior center for their computer class. Fred noticed that his friend was exceptionally chipper. "Hey, Joe, you're in a great mood today."

"I sure am. I got lucky this morning."

"That's really saying something at our age!"

"It sure is—I can barely remember the last time I found the car in the mall parking lot on the first try!"

* * *

Q & A

. . . . .

Q. Where should the old lady look to find flattering and fashionable glasses?

A. On top of her head.

On the way home from their 50th wedding anniversary celebration, the wife notices a tear in her husband's eye and asks if he's getting sentimental because they're celebrating 50 wonderful years together.

He replies, "No, not really.

"I was remembering the time right before we got married when your father threatened me with a shotgun. He caught me kissing you, and you were still 17 at the time, and I had just turned 18. He told me he would have me thrown in jail for 50 years if I didn't marry you, and he scared me half to death, so of course I married you.

"I was just sitting here thinking . . . tomorrow I would've been a free man!"

* * *

You know you're old when restless leg syndrome is the only exercise you get.

* * *

aving gotten the most generous Christmas present she could imagine, Martha beams at her grandmother.

She kisses her on the cheek and says, "Grandma, you are literally an angel!" and then skips away.

"Huh. Not quite yet!" mutters the grandmother after her.

* * *

I'll Have What She's Having

Frank waited patiently in line at the liquor store. When it was his turn, he loudly told the cashier, "Go ahead, card me! That's me, Frank. Today is my 87th birthday, and I'm having a big party at the senior center."

The bored cashier nodded and smiled and went on to the next customer.

Later that afternoon, Frank approached a woman at his party. "Hello. Today's my birthday. I bet you can't guess how old I am."

It wasn't the best pickup line, but the woman took the bait.

"Give me your hand," she said. She studied the lines on his palm carefully and at great length before looking up.

"You're 87 today, and your name is Frank."

"That's incredible! Where did you learn to read palms?"

"Today, when I was standing behind you in line at the liquor store."

*   *   *

Four friends who all had one thing in common—pacemakers—joined a bowling league. Their team name?

We've Got Arrhythms.

*   *   *

Say it Again, Slowly

A retired couple is vacationing in Florida when they wander into a town neither one of them can pronounce, spelled "K-i-s-s-i-m-e-e."

They each try a few different ways to pronounce the odd name, but they cannot agree on which might be correct.

So, when they stop to eat in the town, as they are ordering, the husband explains the couple's dilemma to their server:

"We just can't seem to figure out how to pronounce this place. Will you tell us where we are and say it very slowly and loudly; my wife is hard of hearing."

The server looks at them oddly, then says loudly, "Maaaac Donnnn-aaaald's."

＊　　＊　　＊

Just Passing By

A pair of elderly golfers teams up with a younger pair they had just met at their country club one Sunday morning. As they await their tee-off time, the foursome notices a funeral procession passing by on an adjoining road.

One of the elderly gents separates himself from the group a bit, removes his cap, and bows his head as the procession drives by.

The two younger players remark about how you just don't see respect like that anymore.

The older friend replies:

"Well, after all, it is his wife."

∗   ∗   ∗

*I intend to live forever,
or die trying.*

—GROUCHO MARX

∗   ∗   ∗

At one point during a game, the coach calls one of his 9-year-old baseball players aside and asks, "Do you understand what cooperation is? What a team is?" The little boy nods in the affirmative.

The coach continues, "I'm sure you know, when an out is called, you shouldn't argue, curse, or call the umpire names. Do you understand that?" Again the little boy nods.

He continues, "And when I take you out of the game so another boy gets a chance to play, it's not good sportsmanship to call your coach a moron, is it?" Again the little boy nods.

"Good," says the coach.

"Now go over there and explain all that to your grandmother."

* * *

I really loved the rock band The Kinks back in the 1960s. Now I can't stand even the thought of them.

Their name reminds me of every joint in my body.

*   *   *

GAMES FOR SENIORS

• Simon Did You Say Something?

• Rock-Paper-Carpal Tunnel

• Hops-and-Scotch

• Capture the Bus Seat

• Dodge Bills

• I Spy a Sty in My Eye

• Hide and GPS

I'm In the Mood for Love

A couple in their 40th year of marriage is lying in bed one night, and the husband is nearly asleep; however the wife is in a romantic mood and wants to talk about old times.

"I remember how you always loved to hold my hand when we were courting."

Drowsily, but happily, the husband reaches over, holds his beloved wife's hand for a moment, and then tries to get back to sleep.

It is not to be, however. Just a few moments later she says, "Then you used to kiss me."

Somewhat irritated, he stretches his neck, gives her a sweet little kiss on her cheek, and settles down to sleep again.

Almost immediately, she says, "And then you used to nibble my neck."

Obviously aggravated, the husband gets up out of bed.

"Where are you going, dear?"

"To get my teeth!" is his irritated reply.

✳　✳　✳

I'm a walking file cabinet of fascinating facts.

The only problem is the cabinet seems to be locked, and I have misplaced the key.

✳　✳　✳

Recently I went to the doctor for my annual physical.

The nurse asked me how much I weighed. I told her 135 pounds. Then she weighed me, and the scale said 160.

She asked me how tall I was. I said, "5 feet, 5 inches." She measured me, and I stood only 5′3″.

So she took my blood pressure and told me it was high.

"Of course it's high," I said. "When I came in here I was tall and slender. Now I'm short and fat!"

* * *

I finally have a little money to burn, but my kindling is all burned out.

* * *

You can always pick out the retired basketball players; they dribble a lot more.

* * *

Fred and Edna enjoyed spending Sunday mornings reading tidbits of the paper to each other.

One Sunday, Edna came across this gem: "Fred, it says here that one in four older people suffers from some kind of mental illness. It says to consider your three best friends."

"But none of my three best friends is crazy!"

"Exactly, dear!"

* * *

I want to grow old gracefully.

It turns out, however, that there are quite a few wrinkles in my plan.

* * *

Hearing Test

An elderly woman feared that her husband was going deaf, but she couldn't convince him to see a doctor about it. He just kept insisting that he was fine. So she came up with a test.

She waited until he was sitting in his armchair, then stood behind him all the way across the room and asked, "Honey, when are you going to take out the trash?" When he didn't answer, she stepped a little closer and repeated the process.

She did this a few more times until she was right behind him, and asked one more time, "Honey, when are you going to take out the trash?"

"For the sixth time: TRASH DAY ISN'T UNTIL FRIDAY!" he replied.

* * *

My grandma still drives, bless her heart. Let me describe her for you, so you can watch out for her!

She's the one with both hands white-knuckle gripping the steering wheel, blue hair barely visible above the windshield, driving 35 mph on the highway, alone in the carpool lane, with her right turn signal on for the entire time she's driving.

*   *   *

SENIOR CITIZEN GUIDE TO DAILY ALCOHOL CONSUMPTION

- One drink—good for your heart
- Two drinks—good for your love life
- Three drinks—good for forgetting that you have a heart condition and no love life

Everyone Needs Motivation

An 85-year-old man goes in for his annual checkup, where the doctor proclaims him to be in excellent health. The man stops on his way out the door, hesitates, turns back to the doctor, and asks:

"Doctor, do you think there's a chance I'll live to be 100?"

"Hmm," says the doctor. "It depends. Do you have any bad habits or vices?"

"No," says the man. "I don't smoke, drink, eat red meat, gamble, or sleep around, and I exercise every day."

"Well, sure, you could live to 100, but why would you want to?"

"Because my wife is 22!"

* * *

I wouldn't care, now that I am older, if my mind wandered once in a while.

The thing is, mine gets up and leaves completely sometimes, and very rarely lets me know when it might return.

✳ ✳ ✳

SENIOR SLANG

iPods: Those bluish circles you get from lack of sleep

MySpace: Something everyone needs once in a while

Rebooting: What you do when your husband doesn't take out the trash the first time you ask

During minor surgery, an elderly nun opted to have only a local anesthetic. Afterward, when she was the in recovery room, her nurse came in to ask her how she was feeling.

"Well, I was very disturbed by the four-letter word I heard the doctor use."

"What did he say?" asked the shocked nurse.

"OOPS!"

* * *

Grass the Situation

Four old men are out golfing.

"These hills are getting steeper as the years go by," one complains.

"These fairways seem to be getting longer too," says another.

"The sand traps seem to be bigger than I remember them too," says the third senior.

After hearing enough from his buddies, the oldest, at 87 years old and the wisest of the four, pipes up and says,

"Just be thankful we're still on the right side of the grass!"

*   *   *

My favorite vacation is a trip to Mexico to drink the water.

At my age, Montezuma's revenge is a *relief*.

*   *   *

I got one of those video games that lets you pretend you're bowling.

Now I have to get the new version that lets you pretend you're going to the ER because you threw your back out.

* * *

At my age, I've got all of my money invested in bonds: bonds to hold my teeth in, bonds to hold my hair on, and bonds to keep my car from falling apart.

* * *

I got tired of the neighborhood kids trying to knock my hat off with snowballs, so I had my pharmacist make me a childproof cap.

* * *

A pair of old friends sit in the park shooting the breeze.

"You know what?" says Hank. "Getting old is kind of like being a dog."

"How's that?" asks Chet.

"I'm always excited to see the same old people—even if they leave the room and come back five minutes later!"

* * *

ROD STEWART
SONGS FOR SENIORS

• • • • • • • • • • • • • • • • •

- Itchin' the Night Away
- Street Frightened Man
- You Hear It Well
- Tonight's Too Late
- Hot Restless Legs
- Do Ya Think I'm Breathing?
- Maggie May but Probably Won't Because She's Too Tired

My doctor asked me how I feel, and I said:

"Like a semi truck. It takes me a long time to get going, I go uphill really slow, and I'm pulling a big tank of oxygen."

*　　*　　*

Call Your Mother... and I Don't Mean "Text"

. . . .

I've been plagued by tennis elbow all my life.

When I was young, I got it from playing tennis; now I get it from trying to get the balls to fit on the legs of my walker.

*   *   *

Hold the Phone!

An elderly man in London calls his son who had recently moved to Sydney and says: "I hate to ruin your day, but I have to tell you that your mother and I are divorcing; 45 years of misery is enough.'"

"Dad, what are you talking about?" the son screams.

"We can't stand the sight of each other. I'm sick of talking about this, so call your sister in Los Angeles and tell her," the father adds, then hangs up.

Frantic, the son calls and relates what their father has said.

"I'll take care of this," the sister assures him.

She calls her dad and shouts: "You are not getting divorced! I'm calling my brother back and we'll both be at your house by tomorrow. Until then, you are not to do anything!"

The wise old father turns to his wife and says: "Okay, I've pulled it off. The children are coming home for Christmas and paying their own air fares."

* * *

Over breakfast, three elderly men commiserate with each other.

"I haven't had any action in weeks!" says the first.

"Well, I haven't had any action in months!" says the second.

"I'm going to get some action tonight," boasts the third.

The others look at him suspiciously. "How can you be so sure?"

The third man laughs, "Because I just put three extra doses of fiber powder in my coffee instead of sugar!"

* * *

My grandkids can't understand how I can laugh so hard at movies that don't have any words bleeped out of them.

* * *

If I had known I was going to live this long, I would have waited a few more years before having my midlife crisis.

*   *   *

The difference between young and old is simple:

When you're very young, you need someone to remind you to go to the bathroom.

When you're very old, you need someone who'll tell you when you have gone to the bathroom.

*   *   *

SENIOR DEFINITION

. . . .

SWAT team: a group of old geezers sitting on the porch slapping the mosquitoes off of each other

Lend a Helping Hand

A banker ran into his old friend Roy, an 80-year-old rancher, in town. Roy had lost his wife a year or so before, and rumor had it that he was marrying a "mail order" bride.

Being a good friend, the banker asked Roy if the rumor was true. Roy assured him that it was.

The banker then asked Roy the age of his new bride to be. Roy proudly said, "She'll be 22 in November."

Now the banker, being a wise man, could see that an 80-year-old man could not satisfy the sexual appetite of a young woman. Wanting his old friend's remaining years to be happy, the banker tactfully suggested that Roy should consider getting a hired hand to help him out on the ranch, knowing nature would take its own course.

Roy thought this was a good idea and said he would look for one that afternoon.

About four months later, the banker ran into Roy in town again. "How's the new wife?" asked the banker.

Roy proudly said, "Oh, she's pregnant."

The banker, happy that his sage advice had worked out, continued, "And how's the hired hand?"

Without hesitating, Roy said, "Well, she's pregnant too."

Lying in bed after a passionate encounter, Laurel turns to her husband, Kevin, and sighs. "After all these years, you still have the body of a god!"

"I do?" he asks, surprised and pleased.

"Absolutely. Buddha."

Three ladies meet at the beach to enjoy a beautiful day.

Helen: "My, but it's hot today! It must be 70 out here."

Dottie: "Sunday? No, it's Thursday!"

Annette: "Thirsty? Me too! I told you we should have just skipped the beach and gone right to the cocktails!"

Have you seen the Porsche for seniors?

It's the "I Can't Get Out Of This Thing—Call 911."

* * *

An 83-year-old lady finishes her annual physical examination, whereupon the doctor says, "You are in fine shape for your age, but tell me, do you still have intercourse?"

"Just a minute, I'll have to ask my husband," she says.

She went out to the reception room and says: "Bob, do we still have intercourse?"

Bob answers impatiently, "If I told you once, I told you a thousand times. We have Blue Cross!"

* * *

Wait'll Next Year

Jim sat with his grandchildren watching a Cubs game. He began to get a little melancholy.

"You know, kids," he said, "I'm getting older, and I might not be around long enough to ever see this team win the World Series."

The children were quiet for a while, then little Sally piped up, "Don't worry, Grandpa. Maybe you'll go into extra innings!"

* * *

You may think it's terrible to be "over the hill," but I'm here to tell you:

It's a lot easier on the way down than it was on the way up.

* * *

*A man's only as old as
the woman he feels.*

—GROUCHO MARX

*　　*　　*

After being married for 44 years, Jerry took a careful look at his wife one day and said:

"Forty-four years ago we had a small apartment and a cheap car. We slept on a sofa bed and watched a ten-inch black-and-white TV. But I got to go to bed every night with a hot 25-year-old girl.

"Now, I have a million-dollar home, a $45,000 car, nice big bed, and plasma-screen TV. But...I've got to sleep every night with a 69-year-old woman.

"It seems to me that you're not holding up your side of things."

Jerry's wife is a very reasonable woman.

She told him to go out and find a hot 25-year-old girl, and she would make sure that he would once again be living in a cheap apartment, driving a cheap car, sleeping on a sofa bed, and watching a ten-inch black-and-white TV.

* * *

We thought old Uncle Roy would never retire from being a police officer, but finally one night he just copped out.

*   *   *

For my 85th birthday party I decided to have some fun. After the cake and ice cream, I announced that we were going to play Twister.

Talk about excitement! All the partygoers came running to me with their childproof pill bottles.

*   *   *

You know you're old when you put a laxative in your coffee so you don't fall asleep before you go.

*   *   *

"Grandma, can you remember the name of the boy who gave you your first kiss?"

"Hah! I can't even remember who gave me my last kiss!"

* * *

Two residents of a nursing home are having a dispute over who had chosen the afternoon movie last.

It becomes so heated, that one of them actually shoves the other one down. The head nurse decides to separate the residents when she learns of the scuffle, and to call the police to take a report, for insurance purposes.

It was no use, however. By the time the police arrive, no one, including the witnesses, remembers anything about the incident.

* * *

At the end of the day, two women walk to their cars together. One holds a large shopping bag.

"What's in the bag?" asks the first woman.

"An armchair massage pad. I got it for my husband," replies the second.

After a long pause, she adds: "I definitely got the better end of that deal."

* * *

RAISE YOUR HANDS!

· · · · · · · · · · · · · · · ·

Q. Who really wants to live to be 110, anyway?

A. Anyone who has lived to 109.

It's time people started treating us old folks like bananas and recognizing that those spots just mean we're ripe.

*   *   *

As the doctor completes a thorough examination of his geriatric patient, he says, "I can't find a specific cause for your complaint. To be candid with you, I believe it's because of drinking."

"Well," says the patient, "I'll come back when you've had a chance to sober up a little."

*   *   *

An officer called to the scene of a head-on collision interviews the two drivers. First, he talks to a young woman, who tells him, "That guy was all over the road! I couldn't avoid him."

Then, he walks over to the older man in the second car.

"Sir, the other driver says you were driving erratically."

"I was not! I stayed on my side the entire time!"

"Just out of curiosity, which side was yours?"

"I was just about to make up my mind."

* * *

When I was young I was a good longhaired hippie. Now, however, I long for hair and a good hip.

* * *

Mary and Thelma are old friends. They have both been married to their husbands for a long time; Mary is upset because she thinks her husband doesn't find her attractive anymore.

"As I get older he doesn't bother to look at me!" Mary cries.

"I'm so sorry for you," replies Thelma. "As I get older, my husband says I get more beautiful every day."

"Yes," says Mary, "but your husband's an antique dealer!"

* * *

First you forget names, then you forget faces, then you forget to pull your zipper up, then you forget to pull your zipper down.

—LEO ROSENBERG

* * *

It is always sad when bankers get old and cranky, and they just want to be a loan.

* * *

"Grandpa, why are you always butting in to give me advice?"

"It's because I'm too old now to set a bad example for you, so I'll take what I can get!"

* * *

A Ribbiting Tale

A guy is 81 years old and loves to fish. He is sitting in his boat one day when he hears a voice say, "Pick me up."

He looks around and can't see anyone. He thinks he is dreaming when he hears the voice say again, "Pick me up."

He looks in the water and there, floating on the top, is a frog.

The man says, "Are you talking to me?"

The frog says, "Yes, I'm talking to you. Pick me up. Then kiss me, and I'll turn into the most beautiful woman you have ever seen."

The man looks at the frog for a short time, reaches over, picks it up carefully, and places it in his front breast pocket.

Then the frog says, "What, are you nuts? Didn't you hear what I said? I said kiss me, and I will give you pleasures like you have never had."

He opens his pocket, looks at the frog, and says:

"Nah. At my age I'd rather have a talking frog."

* * *

I don't know much about investing.

The only bond I worry about maturing is the one that's holding my dentures in.

* * *

There's always something to be thankful for if you take the time to look for it.

For example, I was just passing by a mirror, and it occurred to me to be thankful that wrinkles don't hurt.

* * *

Inside every older person is a younger person—wondering what the hell happened.

—CORA HARVEY ARMSTRONG

✳　　✳　　✳

My optometrist caters to seniors on fixed incomes.

His eye chart has only three letters: "I," "O," and "U."

*   *   *

An old man goes to the Wizard to ask him if he can remove a curse the man has been living with for the last 40 years.

The Wizard says, "Maybe, but you will have to tell me the exact words that were used to put the curse on you."

The old man says without hesitation, "I now pronounce you man and wife."

*   *   *

I'm still the life of the party, as long as it is over by 7 P.M.

*   *   *

The hot new exercise for seniors is jogging in the pool.

The only problem is making sure the seniors remember to take their jogging shoes off.

*   *   *

An old gentleman drives in the fast lane of the freeway at his normal cruising speed, which is far too slow.

When the highway patrol officer pulls him over, he asks, "Sir, do you know why I stopped you?"

"Sure I do," the older gent replies.

"I was the only one you could catch!"

* * *

The more you complain, the longer God lets you live.

—ANONYMOUS

* * *

Why are so many retirement villages called Happy Acres? If I'm happy, it means I'm NOT aching.

* * *

You know you're old when "acting your age" would require you to do absolutely nothing.

*   *   *

"My wife is constantly beating me up," my pal Gus admits to me one day.

Concerned, I ask him why.

He says, "I can't hear the alarm clock and she can."

*   *   *

My grandmother was a very tough woman. She buried three husbands—and two of them were just napping.

—RITA RUDNER

*   *   *

The saddest thing I have had to come to grips with in my old age is that brain cells die off, never to return.

Fat cells, however, live forever.

* * *

I'm at the age now where just putting my cigar in its holder is a thrill.

—GEORGE BURNS

*　　*　　*

SITCOMS FOR SENIORS

- Two-and-a-Half Hours of Sleep
- Age 54, Where Are You?
- Everybody Loves Mall Walking
- Grandfather Knows Best
- I Love Loose Slots
- How Did I Meet Your Mother?
- I Dream of Sleeping
- Married with Children and Grand-children Who Don't Call or Write

It's pretty funny to listen to the young guys talk about getting nervous when their doctor puts on a rubber glove.

Wait until they're *my* age; when they go in for their annual checkup, the doctor will put on a rubber suit.

* * *

Thelma had just started down the sidewalk when her friend Janet came around the corner and barreled into her at high speed.

"Slow down, Janet! What's your hurry?"

"Well," puffed Janet, "I read that bee stings can help ease arthritis, so I went out and threw a rock at a big hive in a tree. And then they all started chasing me."

"Must have worked," said Thelma. "I haven't seen you move that quickly since 1974!"

* * *

At Bill's annual checkup, the doctor asks him if he has any concerns.

"I do, Doc," Bill replies. "I'm kind of worried about my memory. I lose my keys all of the time, and sometimes I lose the whole car. I forgot my wife's birthday, and yesterday I even called my grandson by the wrong name. What should I do?"

"Well," says the doctor, "you should start by paying me up front."

* * *

I Can Still Bend Over, but I Don't Have Anything Worth Picking Up

· · · · · · · · · · · · · · · · ·

Two old ladies sit in the beauty parlor, chatting idly as their hair sets.

"Mildred, why do you think they call it a 'permanent' if it grows out so quickly?"

"Well, Judy, I supposed it's that one of these times it will be!"

✳   ✳   ✳

I have enough money to last me the rest of my life, unless I buy something.

—JACKIE MASON

✳   ✳   ✳

As they say, when the age is in, the wit is out.

—WILLIAM SHAKESPEARE

*   *   *

There was once a very famous artist who was visited by a wealthy man. The man requested that the artist, who was getting on in years, paint a portrait of his wife in the nude.

The elderly artist, a very moral man, replied:

"Your offer is a very generous one, however I simply have never done that type of work, and I do not intend to begin in my twilight years."

The wealthy man returned several times however, increasing his offer of payment each time, until the artist finally consented.

"My wife has agreed with me that we do need the money, and I am willing to paint your wife in the nude," the artist said.

"Although I must insist that I be allowed to keep my socks on as I suffer terribly from cold feet."

* * *

You know you're getting old when your naptime and your bedtime have become the same time.

* * *

CLASSIC BOOKS FOR SENIORS

- The Lord of the Ringing Ears
- The Lion, the Witch and How They Stayed Married for 50 Years
- Da Vinci's Cold
- What was the Name of the Rose?
- Harry Potter and the Really Heavy Book
- The Little Prints
- To Kill a Rocking Chair
- What to Expect When You're Expectorating
- Chicken Soup for the Stomach
- A Farewell to Toned Arms

An 80-year-old man goes to the doctor complaining of not being able to get to sleep. His doctor puts him through an entire battery of tests, including lab work, and yet finds no reason why his patient should not be able to sleep properly.

"Mr. Wilson, there is no medical reason for your insomnia," the doctor says. "My suggestion for a good night's sleep is, you need to learn to stop taking your trouble to bed with you."

"Oh, that will never work," answers the old man with a sigh.

"My wife refuses to sleep alone."

*   *   *

My doctor says I need to have more olive oil in my diet.

If olive oil is so good for you, how come Popeye needed to eat all that spinach?

*   *   *

> ## APPLE A DAY
> • • • • • • • • • • •
> I never have any trouble finding my dentures. They're always in the last apple I tried to eat.

The Divine Plan

During the sermon at church one Sunday morning, the priest counseled, "Each and every one of you has a purpose in life, and all you have to do is figure out what God's plan is for you, then try your best to live up to it."

Then he asked for a volunteer to demonstrate. After a long silence, an older man finally got up and went to the front.

"Well, John," said the priest, "surely at your age you have figured out your purpose in life?"

"Yes, Father, I think so."

"Well, what is it?"

John took a deep breath, then blurted out:

"I think I'm here to serve as a warning to everyone else!"

* * *

I used to get my car "winterized" and "summerized." Now I get it "seniorized."

The mechanic at the garage makes sure my seat is up high, the radio is permanently tuned to AM, and the jumper cables have defibrillator pads.

* * *

My grandkids want me to get something called a "smart phone."

When I was their age, a smart phone was one on a land line that you could unplug when the neighbor was calling to find out who broke her window with a baseball.

$$* \quad * \quad *$$

Don't Be Chicken

A farmer is retiring, selling his land, and giving away his stock of animals to all his neighbors. He has a sly sense of humor: He devises a plan to give a horse to the houses where the husband is the boss, and a chicken to the houses where the woman is the boss.

The farmer arrives at a small farm where the couple is outside doing some weeding.

"Who's the boss around here?" the farmer asks. "I am," replies the husband.

"Great, I have a white horse and a black horse to give away," the farmer states. "Which one would you like?"

The husband considers it for just a moment and says, "Why thank you, I'll take the black one."

"Oh no you don't. We want the white one," the man's wife says abruptly.

"Okay. Here's your chicken," says the farmer.

* * *

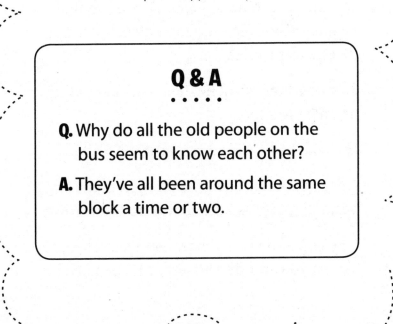

Q & A
· · · · ·

Q. Why do all the old people on the bus seem to know each other?

A. They've all been around the same block a time or two.

Bury the Hatchet

A man and woman were married for many years, even though they hated each other. When they had a confrontation, screaming and yelling could be heard deep into the night.

The old man would shout, "When I die, I will dig my way up out of the grave and come back and haunt you!"

Neighbors feared him because of the many strange occurrences that took place in their neighborhood. The old man liked the fact that he was feared.

To everyone's relief, he died of a heart attack when he was 78.

His wife had a closed casket at the wake.

After the burial, she went straight home and began to party as if there was no tomorrow.

One concerned neighbor, however, asked, "Aren't you afraid that he may indeed be able to dig his way up out of the grave and come back and haunt you?"

The wife said:

"Let the old man dig. I had him buried upside down."

* * *

Socked In

Two elderly friends are sitting on a bench waiting for their bus. The bus is running very late, and a lot of time has passed.

After a while, one woman begins to shift around a bit and says, "You know, we've been sitting here so long, my bottom fell asleep!"

Her friend replies rather sarcastically:

"Oh, I know! I heard it snoring!"

* * *

Horse Hockey

A little old lady answers a knock on the door, only to be confronted by a well-dressed young man carrying a vacuum cleaner.

"Good morning," says the young man. "If I could take a couple of minutes of your time, I would like to demonstrate the very latest in high-powered vacuum cleaners."

"Go away!" says the old lady. "I haven't got any money!" and she proceeds to close the door.

Quick as a flash, the young man wedges his foot in the door and pushes it wide open. "Don't be too hasty!" he says.

"Not until you have at least seen my demonstration."

And with that, he empties a bucket of horse manure onto her hallway carpet. "If this vacuum cleaner does not remove all traces of this horse manure from your carpet, I will personally eat the remainder."

The old lady steps back and says:

"Well then, I hope you've got a very good appetite, because they cut off my electricity this morning!"

* * *

Two elderly couples are enjoying some friendly conversation when one of the men asks the other, "Hey, Henry, how was the memory clinic you attended last month?"

"Amazing," he replies. "Why I learned all the latest techniques in visualization, association, and the like. It made a real difference in my memory."

"That's terrific, what was the name of the clinic?"

Henry is embarrassed. For the life of him, he cannot remember.

Then a smile breaks across his face and he asks, "What do you call that flower with the long stem and thorns?"

"You mean a rose?"

"Yes, that's it!" He turns to his wife:

"Rose, what was the name of that memory clinic?"

* * *

I heard they did not even throw a retirement party for old man Hamilton after 47 years at the sewage plant.

I guess he just wasted away.

*　　*　　*

Time may be a great healer, but it sure makes a lousy mirror.

*　　*　　*

Two elderly friends are eating breakfast in a restaurant, when Vern notices something unusual about Jerry's ear. He says, "Jerry, why in the world do you have a suppository stuck in your left ear?"

"Oh, for Pete's sake!" Jerry reaches up, pulls out the suppository and looks at it.

Then he says rather glumly:

"Well, I guess I can stop looking for my hearing aid now."

*　　*　　*

Q & A

· · · · ·

Q: What's the best way to slow down the aging process?

A: Pass it through Congress.

As you get older, the pickings get slimmer, but the people don't.

—CARRIE FISHER

*　　*　　*

Three old men are working out and bragging about their love lives.

"I don't know what it is about getting older, but my wife and I only make love once a month now," complains Tom.

"Really? Because my wife and I make love once a week," replies Phil.

"Oh yeah?" says Don. "My wife and I come close to making love every night."

Tom and Phil turn to Don as he continues:

"We come close to it on Monday night; we come close to it on Tuesday night…."

*　　*　　*

An archaeologist is the best husband a woman can have. The older she gets the more interested he is in her.

—AGATHA CHRISTIE

* * *

A 65-year-old woman marries a much younger man, and they decide to adopt a baby. One day, when he is at work, some of their relatives come to visit.

When they ask to see the baby, the elderly mother replies, "Not yet" several times, until she is asked when the baby can be seen.

"Oh, you will all see her when she cries," answers the aging mother.

"Why do we have to wait until the baby cries," asks one of the relatives. The mother says:

"Well, that's how I find where I left her."

*　*　*

Old guys never like to admit they own cats.

If you see one at the store buying cans of cat food, he'll tell you he's in a senior hockey league and they're cheaper than pucks.

*　*　*

My friend Marge went to an acupuncturist for her headaches.

It didn't help her migraines, but she told him to leave the needles in her forehead anyway.

It was cheaper than a face-lift.

* * *

Don't worry about avoiding temptation ... as you grow older, it will avoid you.

—WINSTON CHURCHILL

* * *

How many grannies does it take to change a lightbulb?

Two; one to take out the old bulb, and one to organize a bus trip to an outlet mall that sells cheap bulbs.

* * *

Q & A
· · · · ·

Q: How many little old men does it take to change a lightbulb?

A: None. Who's still up when it's dark?

A married couple was celebrating their 60th wedding anniversary. At the party everybody wanted to know how they managed to stay married so long in this day and age.

The husband responded, "When we were first married we came to an agreement. I would make all the major decisions and my wife would make all the minor decisions."

At which point the wife took up the tale:

"And, in 60 years of marriage, we have never needed to make a major decision."

* * *

With Whipped Cream

A couple who are both in their nineties are having problems remembering things. After they get a checkup, the doctor tells them that they're physically okay, but they might want to start writing things down to help them remember.

Later that night while watching TV, the old man gets up from his chair. His wife asks, "Where are you going?" "To the kitchen," he replies. "Will you get me a bowl of ice cream?" "Sure."

"Don't you think you should write it down so you can remember it?" she asks.

"No, I can remember it."

"Well, I'd like some strawberries and whipped cream on top, too. You'd better write it down because you know you'll forget it."

Irritated, he says, "I don't need to write it down, I can remember it! Ice cream with strawberries and whipped cream—I got it, for goodness sake!"

After about 20 minutes, the old man returns from the kitchen and hands his wife a plate of bacon and eggs.

She stares at the plate for a moment, then says, "Where's my toast?"

YOU KNOW YOU'RE OLD WHEN...

• • • • • • • • • • •

- You say you want to *befriend* some-one, rather than *friend* them—and you do it in person, rather than on Facebook.

- You have no idea what an Apatosaurus is, but you wonder why the kids don't learn about the mighty Brontosaurus anymore.

- "Act your age, not the speed limit" is suddenly a compliment.

- You have less hair on your head, but more in your nose, ears, and eyebrows.

- People begin calling you "Sir," but you're not a knight.

A woman approaches an older lady at the gym and says, "I have to tell you: It's just an inspiration the way you're always smiling at everyone."

The old lady says, "What's that, dear? You'll have to speak up."

"I said I think it's great that you're always smiling."

"Oh, thank you. That's because I can't hear what anyone is saying."

*   *   *

Young men think old men are fools; but old men know young men are fools.

—GEORGE CHAPMAN

*   *   *

You know you're a senior when the high point of your birthday party is getting the last candle lit before the first one burns a hole through your cake.

* * *

"Grandma, back when you were in school, did you have to take History class?"

"No, honey; back then, we took *Making History* class!"

* * *

The idea is to die young
as late as possible.

—ASHLEY MONTAGU

*　　*　　*

On the phone with her best friend, Mabel indulges in a pity party.

"I just feel so old, Joan! I've gained weight, my energy is down, I find new wrinkles and gray hairs in the mirror every day, and let's not even talk about the hairs that are sprouting in other places!

"Quick—tell me something good about myself to make me feel better."

Without thinking, Joan replies:

"Well, your attention to detail is still as sharp as ever!"

*　　*　　*

Ask Not What Your Wife Can Do for You…

One day, a retired scientist was talking to his friend, a retired psychologist. The scientist had noticed, since he had so much more time at home, how inefficiently things were run around the house, and he thought it would make a good project for him to increase the efficiency.

"I'm going to start with lunch," the scientist told his friend. "It takes my wife half an hour to get lunch on the table, and with a few simple solutions, she could easily cut that time in half."

"Hmm," said the psychologist, "what did you have in mind?"

"Well, for example, she brings things from the kitchen to the dining room one at a time. If she could carry more at once, it would definitely be more efficient. I think I'll talk to her about it today."

The psychologist could barely muffle his laughter. "Let me know how it works out for you."

The next day, the psychologist came upon the scientist, who was looking quite glum.

"How did it go?" he asked.

"Well, it's definitely more efficient. Now it takes me only ten minutes to make my own lunch."

*　　*　　*

You can't help getting older, but you don't have to get old.

—GEORGE BURNS

*　　*　　*

If God had wanted me to hear better at my age, he would have given me bigger hands.

*　　*　　*

Y ou know you are over the hill when your back goes out more than you do.

* * *

The older the fiddle the sweeter the tune.

—PABLO PICASSO

SENIOR DEFINITION

• • • • • • • • • • • • •

Yahoo: Someone who thinks looking something up on the Internet is more fun than going to the library.

At her annual checkup, the doctor tells Mary that she needs to eat more fresh fruits and vegetables.

Mary replies, "No way! At my age, I need all the preservatives I can get!"

* * *

I got a set of golf clubs designed just for senior golfers. It has an extra-long putter so I don't have to bend over when I beat it on the ground after missing a short one.

* * *

"Old" Is the New "Ancient"

· · · · · · · · · · · · · · ·

My great-uncle Bob is 14 years younger than my great-aunt Helen, and he never lets her forget it. Last week, an unknown solicitor phoned. As soon as Uncle Bob got off the phone, Aunt Helen walked in the room and asked who had called.

Always the prankster, Uncle Bob replied:

"It was the University, dear, and they were inquiring about you donating your body to science.

"They are desperate for specimens of ancient civilizations."

* * *

I have flabby thighs, but fortunately my stomach covers them.

—JOAN RIVERS

* * *

I hate getting shorter every year.

I may be old, but I still like to ride roller coasters.

* * *

These new digital photo albums are not for seniors.

They take all the fun out of drawing mustaches on relatives you don't like.

*   *   *

Car 54, Where Are You?

The old guy down the block, George, was going up to bed when his wife told him that he'd left the light on in the garden shed. George opened the back door to go turn off the light but saw that there were people in the shed stealing things.

He phoned the police, who asked, "Is someone in your house?"

He said, "No, but some people broke into my garden shed and are stealing from me."

Then the police dispatcher said, "All patrols are busy. Lock your doors and someone will be along when one is available."

George hung up the phone, counted to 30, and phoned the police again.

"Hello, I just called you because there were people stealing things from my shed. Well, you don't have to worry about them now because I just shot them." Then he hung up.

Within three minutes, six police cars, a SWAT team, and an ambulance showed up at George's residence, catching the burglars red-handed.

One of the cops said to George, "I thought you said that you'd shot them!"

George said, "I thought you said there was nobody available!"

*　　*　　*

My hands have so many liver spots they now all have sides of onions and bacon with them.

*　　*　　*

Breaking the Law

After looking for the best one they could afford, a family brought their mother to a nursing home. On her first day there, the frail woman was bathed, fed a nice breakfast, and then set near a window with a lovely view.

She seemed comfortably propped up, however she soon began to lean over to one side. When an attentive aide noticed it, she rushed to straighten her, and placed a pillow on the side where the woman was slipping.

A short time later, the woman began to slip again, this time in the other direction. Once again, an aide caught her and propped her back upright. This went on all day.

That evening the woman's family came to visit her and ask how her first day went. "Tell us the truth Mother: How is it here?"

"Well, everyone here is very kind, the food is fine, and as you can see it is very clean," she said. But then she continued:

"But, for heaven's sake, they must have some crazy rule about not letting anyone pass gas!"

* * *

I always use the valet parking whenever the service is available.

Never once has that nice young man forgotten where he parked my car.

* * *

I went to buy a new easy chair and realized that the people who design cars should be put in charge of designing furniture.

My front seat is the perfect lounge chair—it's soft and heated, there's a cup holder so my drink doesn't spill out, and there's a seat belt so *I* don't spill out.

* * *

I noticed I spend a lot more time these days wondering about the hereafter.

I go somewhere to get something, and then wonder what I'm here after.

* * *

A grandmother is watching her grandchild playing on the beach when a huge wave comes and takes him out to sea.

She pleads, "Please God, save my only grandson! I beg of you, bring him back."

And a big wave comes and washes the boy back onto the beach, good as new.

The grandmother looks up to heaven and says: "He had a hat!"

Q & A

Q. Why do so many old folks drive big cars?

A. Try spending 30 minutes strapping your walker to the top of a subcompact, and you'll find out.

I know I'm getting old because lately my knees have begun to buckle, but my belt won't.

* * *

I don't get social media. At my age, "my space page" is the newspaper I read in the bathroom.

* * *

*Age seldom arrives smoothly
or quickly. It's more often
a succession of jerks.*

—JEAN RHYS

*　*　*

There was a man who was 82, married to a woman who was 80. One day, the woman came home from shopping only to find her husband sleeping with a 30-year-old woman. The wife picked up her husband and threw him out of the window.

When the police came, one cop asked the woman. "Why didn't you just divorce your husband?"

And the wife replied: "Well, I figured if he could do that at his age, then he could fly, too."

*　*　*

It's a Little More Serious than I First Thought

Two medical students would often place small wagers between themselves, trying to determine what was wrong with a patient just by observing them for a short while.

One day they spotted an old fellow sort of duck-waddling down the hospital hall. The two students introduced themselves to the elderly gentleman and explained that they didn't agree with each other's diagnosis of his problem.

The first one said, "My friend thinks you have a severe case of hemorrhoids, however I am sure you are suffering with a hernia. Would you please tell us which one of us is correct?"

The old man shifted around uncomfortably and replied:

"Well fellows, I thought it was just gas, but it seems as though we were all wrong!"

*   *   *

Our favorite restaurant tried to get cute by putting the time of the early-bird special in Roman numerals.

At 4 P.M., there was a line out front of people waiting for bottles to hook up to their IVs.

*   *   *

The secret of staying young is to live honestly, eat slowly, and lie about your age.

—LUCILLE BALL

*   *   *

Old gardeners never die; they just go to seed.

*   *   *

Take It to the Limit

A state police officer noticed a car puttering along the main highway at only 22 mph. He turned on his siren and pulled the car over. As he approached the driver, he observed that the vehicle contained five elderly ladies.

Two were in the front seat, and there were three more in the back. The officer noticed that all the passengers looked terrified; however, the driver seemed merely confused.

"Officer, I don't understand. I wasn't speeding, was I?"

"No, Ma'am," the officer replied, "In fact, you were actually going so slow that you could be a danger to other drivers."

"Slower than the speed limit? No, I'm following the posted speed exactly. Look there, 22 mph!"

The officer, trying not to laugh, explained "22" was the highway number, not the speed limit. Embarrassed, the woman thanked the officer for pointing out her error.

Before letting her go, however, the officer asked, "Is everyone in the car okay? Your passengers look like they've seen a ghost!"

"Oh, they'll calm down in a minute, officer. We just got off Highway 95."

* * *

On the way out to a party, Emily notices that her grandmother is carrying an umbrella, raincoat, and rain boots. Curious, she asked, "Grandma, the sky is perfectly clear. Did you see something on the TV weather forecast?"

"Weather forecast? With these joints, I don't even need to turn on the television!"

*　　*　　*

SENIOR SLANG

Emoticon: Something manipulative grand-children do to increase their inheritance

Wii: A French video game

Googling: Looking someone over in a very inappropriate way

Shirley, an elderly woman, was telling her friend Carol about her date with a 90-year-old man. "Can you believe it? I had to slap him three times just during dinner!" laughed Shirley.

"You do not mean to tell me that old man tried to get fresh with you?" Carol asked with disgust.

"Oh heavens no, dear," explained Shirley. "I was just slapping him around every once in a while to keep him awake!"

*   *   *

I Can't Drive 55

A Florida senior citizen drove his brand-new Corvette convertible out of the dealership. Taking off down the road, he pushed it to 80 mph, enjoying the wind blowing through what little hair he had left.

"Amazing," he thought as he flew down the highway, pushing the pedal even more.

Looking in his rearview mirror, he saw the state trooper behind him, blue lights flashing and siren blaring. He floored it to 100 mph, then 110, then 120.

Suddenly he thought, "What am I doing? I'm too old for this," and pulled over to await the trooper's arrival.

Pulling in behind him, the trooper walked up to the Corvette, looked at his watch and said, "Sir, my shift ends in 30 minutes. Today is Friday. If you can give me a reason for speeding that I've never heard before, I'll let you go."

The old gentleman paused, then said:

"Three years ago, my wife ran off with a Florida State Trooper. I thought you were bringing her back."

"Have a good day, sir," replied the trooper.

* * *

Two golden-agers were having a cup of tea one afternoon, discussing their husbands.

"I do wish that my Elmer would stop biting his nails. He makes me terribly nervous."

"My Billy used to do the same thing," the older woman replied. "But I broke him of the habit."

"How?"

"I hid his teeth."

*   *   *

"Oh no, another text from my granddaughter," said Marcia. "What's wrong with that?" asked Bob.

"The screens are so small and I can't see very well."

"No problem," said Bob. "I can read it for you."

So Bob took the cell phone, read the message, smiled, and then snapped the phone shut and handed it back to Marcia. A minute passed.

"Well," said Marcia, "what did it say?"

"What did *what* say?"

*　　*　　*

ROLLING STONES SONGS FOR SENIORS

- "Get Off of My Couch"
- "19th Hip Replacement"
- "You Can't Always Hear What You Want"
- "Beast of Burpin'"
- "Wake Me Up"
- "Sympathy Card for the Devil"
- "I Can't Get No Bowel Reaction"

Knock on Wood

Three spinster sisters were sitting around their dining table, discussing the various ways age had caught up with them.

The first one admitted her memory was getting so bad she would stop on the stairs and forget if she was headed up or down sometimes.

The next sister remarked that her memory was really getting bad, because she had put the mail in the fridge and set a sandwich in the mailbox.

The other sisters laughed, however the third sister said, "Well, I may have a few little complaints about aging, however my memory is just fine, knock wood," as she gave the table a rap with her knuckles.

Then she jumped up to see who was at the door.

* * *

I'm at that age when I have seen it all ... and I've done it all.

The problem is, I can't remember most of it!

* * *

We never thought Grandpa would give up his plumbing business, but then suddenly his health really went down the drain.

* * *

We All Have Our Priorities

Joanne, a rather stylish lady in her day, is standing at the rail of the cruise ship holding her hat so that it won't blow away in the wind.

Howard, an older gentleman, approaches her rather awkwardly and says, "Pardon me, madam, I do not know how to say this; however, are you aware that your dress is being dreadfully blown about in this wind?"

"Yes, thank you, I know," replies Joanne, "However as much as that may embarrass me, I must attend to my hat."

"But madam," insists Howard, "Surely you realize your entire rear end is being exposed at times!"

Joanne looks squarely at Howard, and retorts:

"Kind sir, anything you may see down there is 85 years old, but I just bought this hat yesterday!"

* * *

Q & A

· · · · ·

Q. Which came first, the chicken or the egg?

A. Who cares? I may not be a spring chicken, but I'm not totally cracked yet, either!

I accidentally sat on my passport and then spilled some coffee on it, and the photo got all wrinkly and spotted.

Now I don't have to get a new one taken.

*   *   *

Wisdom doesn't necessarily come with age. Sometimes age just shows up all by itself.

—TOM WILSON

*   *   *

*When you become senile,
you won't know it.*

—BILL COSBY

* * *

You know you're old when instead of look-ing forward to going to a new, hip joint, you're looking forward to getting a new hip joint.

* * *

When my eyesight wasn't as good as it used to be, I got a GPS so I could still drive my car.

Guess I probably should have gotten a hearing aid before I used it!

* * *

A Very Awkward First Date

Woman: "Do you have all your own teeth?"

Man: "Yes. Would you like to see the receipt?"

* * *

I grew up in an age when all proper young ladies carried purses, and I can't stand it when I see girls today with all of their stuff crammed in a back pocket.

I guess that makes me "lack totes intolerant."

* * *

Everybody makes fun of us old guys who have our pants pulled up to our armpits.

You won't laugh when you get to our age and find out what it's like to have freezing nipples.

* * *

The old believe everything; the middle aged suspect everything; the young know everything.

—OSCAR WILDE

* * *

My doctor told me I have to really watch my salt intake.

I'm not even allowed to listen to old sailors swear.

* * *

A man was turning 100 years old, and a young reporter had been invited to the celebration.

"Sir, all my readers are going to want to know the secret to your long life," the reporter said, adding: "Please tell me how you managed to live so long?"

"Well, it's like this, sonny," began the old man. "I got married right after I turned 21. The wife and I did not believe in divorce, and we decided early on that if there were ever an argument between us, the one who lost would take a good long walk until they figured out what they had done wrong, and were sorry.

"Yep, I suppose I would have to credit 79 years of nearly daily long walks to my good health and long life."

* * *

Up the River in the Same Boat

Two men snuck out of the nursing home to enjoy a night of poker and cigars. When they went to sneak back in, they found the entrance blocked by two women having a leisurely chat.

"I can't go in there!" said the first man. "One of those women is my wife, and the other is my girlfriend. You'll have to distract them so I can sneak by."

"Sure thing, buddy, I've got you covered," replied the second man. He walked toward the nursing home, then abruptly turned and came back.

"What's the matter?"

"Small world."

* * *

Bill showed up to his family reunion in a new convertible, with a much younger woman at his side.

"Ah," said one cousin to another. "I see Great-Uncle Bill has hit his three-quarter-life crisis!"

* * *

I don't want to tell you how much insurance I carry with the Prudential, but all I can say is: when I go, they go too.

—JACK BENNY

*   *   *

It'll Be Our "Secret"

At bridge club meetings, the members often noticed that Betty had a mysterious white ring in her hair. It started at her bangs and went in a circle all around her head.

The other members, not wanting to be rude, never said anything about it to Betty's face, but often discussed it amongst themselves. No one could figure out what it could be.

Then, after one meeting Betty's daughter came to pick her up and the mystery was solved. "Seriously, Mom? You sprayed your antiperspirant instead of hairspray again!"

The other club members immediately decided that the moral of the story was:

"Speak softly, and carry deodorant in a stick."

*   *   *

Q & A
· · · · ·

Q: What's the longest sentence known to man?

A: I do.

Grandpa went to the doctor for a visit. "Can you do something about the stiffness in my neck?" he asked the doctor. "Of course I can," said the physician. "I'll prescribe a pill that will make it go away."

"I don't want it to go away," Grandpa told him. "I just want it to move a little lower."

*   *   *

The couple knew their parents were still getting frisky when they made a surprising discovery: The handrail they had installed in the bedroom for them had been unscrewed and was now in a vertical position over the bed.

*   *   *

Married men live longer than single men. But married men are a lot more willing to die.

—JOHNNY CARSON

*   *   *